HOW YOUR BODY WORKS

Getting Energy

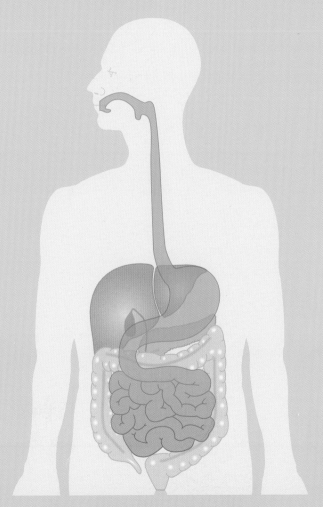

by Philip Morgan

AMICUS

Published by Amicus
P.O. Box 1329, Mankato, Minnesota 56002

Printed in the United States of America at Corporate Graphics, in North Mankato, Minnesota.

Library of Congress Cataloging-in-Publication Data
Morgan, Philip, 1948 Oct. 16-
  Getting energy / Philip Morgan.
      p. cm. -- (How your body works)
  Includes index.
  Summary: "Discusses the different ways the body produces energy"--Provided by publisher.
  ISBN 978-1-60753-053-4 (library binding)
  1. Energy metabolism--Juvenile literature. I. Title.
  QP176.M67 2011
  612.3'9--dc22

                    2009047340

Created by Appleseed Editions Ltd.
Designed by Helen James
Edited by Mary-Jane Wilkins
Artwork by Graham Rosewarne
Picture research by Su Alexander
Consultant: Steve Parker

Photograph acknowledgements
page 4 A Inden/Corbis; 5 Awilli/Corbis; 6 Maximilian Stock Ltd/Science Photo Library; 7 Charles &
Josette Lenars/Corbis; 8 Jose Luis Pelaez/Blend Images/Corbis; 11 Eye of Science/Science Photo Library;
12 Steve Gschmeissner/Science Photo Library; 13 Biomedical Imaging Unit, Southampton General
Hospital/Science Photo Library; 15 Gastrolab/Science Photo Library; 16 Steve Gschmeissner/Science
Photo Library; 17 Saturn Stills/Science Photo Library; 21 Steve Gschmeissner/Science Photo Library;
23 (top) Thomas Deerinck,NCMIR/Science Photo Library, (bottom) Hybrid Medical Animation/Science
Photo Library; 24 Drew Kelly Photography/Corbis; 25 Larry Williams/Corbis; 26 Claus Lunau/Bonnier
Publications/Science Photo Library; 27 Science Photo Library; 28 A Crump, TDR,WHO/Science Photo
Library; 29 AJ Photo/HPR Bullion/Science Photo Library
Front cover Fred de Noyelle/Godong/Corbis

DAD0037
32010

9 8 7 6 5 4 3 2 1

Contents

What Is Energy For?

Your muscles need energy—without it, they wouldn't be able to move, but your muscles are not the only parts of your body that use energy. Every cell in your body needs energy to work well.

The natural sugar in fruit, such as apples, helps to provide energy.

Giving You Power

Your muscles use lots of energy to produce the power they need to contract, or get shorter, and extend. When you concentrate on solving a problem, the nerve cells in your brain use energy to power your thoughts.

Energy and power are essential for the cells in all your organs and tissues, including your heart, kidneys, bones, liver, lungs, eyes, ears, teeth, and skin.

Eating and Breathing

Your body gets energy from the food you eat using oxygen from the air you breathe. Getting energy involves chemicals that your body makes and your blood carries to your cells. The energy in your cells comes from burning fuel, although it doesn't burn in the same way as wood or coal, which make flames. The fuel that your cells burn is a chemical called **glucose**. This is a simple sugar you get from digested food.

The oxygen you breathe is important, too. It needs to reach your cells at the same time as the glucose. Glucose and oxygen are carried around your body in your blood, but the real action takes place inside your cells. They release energy when they burn glucose, with the help of oxygen.

Different Chemicals

Your body contains many different chemicals, which are called molecules. Molecules of water are the ones you have the most of. You have probably heard of others, such as **carbohydrates**, **fats**, **proteins**, and **vitamins**, because these are in your food.

Every time you exercise, such as jumping rope, you burn glucose to make energy.

BREAKING DOWN AND BUILDING UP

Every second your body is breaking down large **molecules**, such as carbohydrates, into smaller ones, such as glucose. It also combines smaller molecules to make bigger ones, such as proteins. The way your body breaks down some molecules and builds up others is called **metabolism**.

The Fuel Your Body Burns

Your body needs a supply of glucose and oxygen just to stay alive. Glucose comes from the food you eat and oxygen from the air you breathe. The oxygen allows your cells to burn glucose, which produces water and carbon dioxide—and releases energy.

Cereal, whole grain bread, pasta, potatoes, and rice all contain complex carbohydrates.

Where Does Glucose Come From?

Most of the glucose your body uses comes from the carbohydrates in the food you eat. Foods such as bread, rice, and potatoes contain a complex carbohydrate called **starch**. Your **saliva** (see pages 10–11) and stomach break this down into glucose. Other foods, such as sugar and honey, contain simple carbohydrates that your stomach can turn into glucose.

Your liver keeps a big store of glucose in its cells. It turns the glucose into a complex carbohydrate called **glycogen**. When your body needs a lot of glucose, the liver breaks down the glycogen into glucose and sends it around your body in your blood.

What Else Can You Burn?

When you don't have enough glucose and your supply of glycogen is low, your cells may start to burn fats. Fats can give you more energy than glucose, because fats contain more **calories** (see pages 24–25).

TYPES OF SUGAR

There are many types of sugars in the food you eat. Table sugar, for example, contains **sucrose**. The sugar in fruit is called fructose, and the sugar in milk is called **lactose**. Your body changes all of these sugars into glucose and burns them to give you energy.

WHEN THINGS GO WRONG

Not Enough Food

People who are starving have burned all the fat in their bodies and then start to burn their protein. Burning protein gives you about the same amount of energy as burning carbohydrates. It is bad for your body because proteins form all the structures in your body, especially muscles. People with **malnutrition** (see page 28) do not have enough to eat. Their bodies have very little fat and have to burn protein for energy.

Peaches, pears, pomegranates, and other fruits all contain simple sugars, such as fructose.

Feeling Hungry

After you have eaten a meal, you feel full. A lot of blood goes to your stomach and intestines as you digest and absorb the carbohydrates, fats, and proteins that you have eaten. After a few hours of moving around and using energy you start to feel hungry again, and then you want to eat more food.

Hunger Pains

When you're hungry, you get a feeling in your stomach known as pangs of hunger. This sensation of hunger starts after many hours without eating and is caused by your stomach muscles contracting strongly. Sometimes, you feel so hungry, it's almost painful. When you're very hungry, you can't do anything else except get some food and eat it!

Eating a good meal with your family is better than snacking!

Did You Know?

During your lifetime, you will probably eat and digest about 66,140 pounds (30,000 kg) of food—the same weight as six full-grown male elephants!

Hunger starts when the brain tells the stomach to contract (red arrow). Eating a meal puts food in your stomach, which sends a message to the brain (green arrow) to turn off the hunger signal.

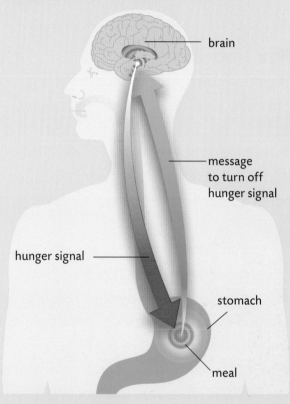

brain

message to turn off hunger signal

hunger signal

stomach

meal

In ancient times, a Stone Age hunter had to go out and kill an animal for food before he and his family could eat. Today, many people in the world go hungry because they don't have enough to eat and cannot afford to buy food. You are probably lucky: all you have to do is go to the refrigerator and grab whatever you want.

What Makes You Hungry?

Many families eat breakfast, lunch, and dinner at about the same time every day. One reason you feel pangs of hunger before a meal is that your body expects to eat. Another reason is that your stomach is empty. You also feel pangs when the amount of sugar in your blood falls below a certain level, which sends a signal to your brain that you need to eat (see above right).

An Appetite

When you are expecting to eat, your mouth and stomach produce digestive juices that give you a pleasant feeling known as appetite. The smell and sight of food can also produce these juices.

Sometimes, a person completely loses his or her appetite and can't eat anything. This problem can lead to an illness called **anorexia**.

Digesting Food

Your body can digest almost any food—from hamburgers and raw fish to cabbage, ice cream, and peanuts. Powerful chemicals in your **digestive system** break down the food into small particles, and then your body absorbs as much as it can.

Mix and Mash

Digestion starts in your mouth. When you chew your food, your teeth, tongue, and jaws mix and mash it with your saliva. This liquid contains strong chemicals that start to break down carbohydrates, called starches, into smaller pieces.

When the food has become a gooey ball, you swallow it in a gulp that pushes it down a tube called your **esophagus** (i-sof-a-gus). This tube has muscles that tighten and loosen in waves, and push the ball of food into your stomach. From the moment you swallow, the food takes about six seconds to reach your stomach.

The food you eat starts its journey in your mouth, then travels down the esophagus to your stomach. As it moves into your small intestine, it mixes with juices from the pancreas and gallbladder.

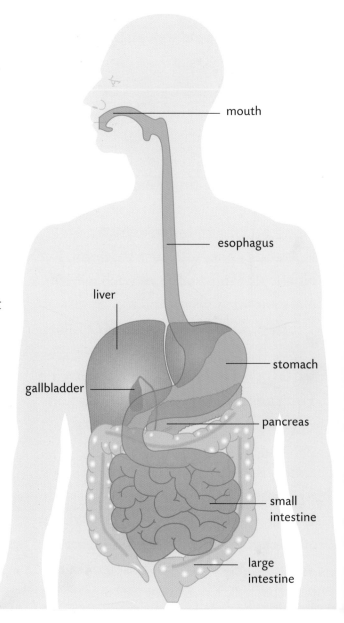

mouth

esophagus

liver

gallbladder

stomach

pancreas

small intestine

large intestine

The lining of the stomach near the opening to the small intestine has many folds, where a slimy liquid called mucus is made.

Inside Your Stomach

As you eat a meal, all the balls of food you swallow collect in your stomach, which grows bigger as more food arrives and is churned up. The stomach walls produce a powerful chemical to kill **bacteria** that enter with the food. Your stomach also makes a slimy liquid, called **mucus**, to protect the stomach walls from the powerful chemical.

Moving On

The churned-up food in your stomach is called **chyme**. After two to four hours, the chyme starts to leave your stomach and goes into your small intestine. Here, the food is mixed with more juices that help to break the food down into simpler chemicals. Some of the juices come from the small intestine, and others from an organ called the pancreas.

A yellowish-green liquid, called **bile**, also helps to break down the fatty substances in the chyme while it is in your small intestine. This bile comes from a small pouch called your **gallbladder**.

How Your Body Absorbs Food

As you digest the chyme, it passes along your small intestine, which has leaky walls to allow the nutrients from the chyme to pass through them into your blood.

A Huge Area

The wall of your small intestine is not flat—it has millions of tiny, finger-like folds, called villi. Each of these has lots of smaller folds, called microvilli. All these sticking-out pieces make a huge area that can absorb the chemicals, or nutrients, from the chyme into your blood. They also absorb quite a lot of water.

Your small intestine is about 7.6 yards (7 m) long, but the villi give it an area of about 299 square yards (250 sq m). Tiny blood vessels in the villi and microvilli absorb the nutrients from chyme, and take them along a larger blood vessel to your liver. What's left of the food goes from the small intestine into the large intestine.

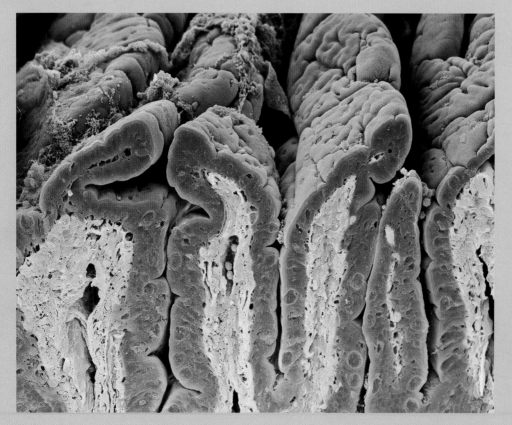

The lining of the small intestine has millions of deep folds, called villi, that absorb chemicals from the food (pink at top).

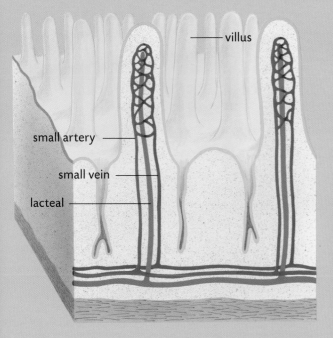

villus

small artery

small vein

lacteal

Each villus has its own blood supply, and a vessel, called a lacteal, to collect fat.

Did You Know?

Almost half the weight of your feces is made up of dead bacteria.

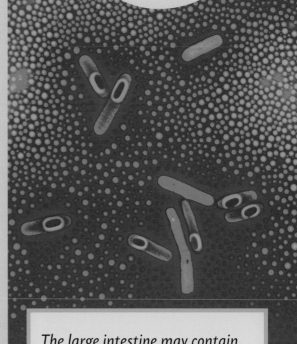

The large intestine may contain many bacteria, such as the rod-shaped bacteria known as E. coli.

Good Bacteria

Various kinds of bacteria grow in the colon, which is the main part of the large intestine. We call them "good" bacteria, because they help your body make some vitamins, which are absorbed into your blood. The bacteria also defend your body against harmful organisms, although they die when they do this.

A Sugar Boost

When you eat a sugary snack, such as a chocolate bar, or drink something sugary, such as soda, your body quickly absorbs the sugars they contain. The level of glucose in your blood rises fast, giving you an energy boost. But the boost doesn't last long, and once it is used up, the amount of glucose in your blood falls quickly, leaving you with very little energy.

Getting Rid of Waste

What happens to the slushy, liquid chyme after the intestines have absorbed everything they can? It slowly moves through the large intestine, and is gradually turned into feces. You push them out of your body when you go to the bathroom.

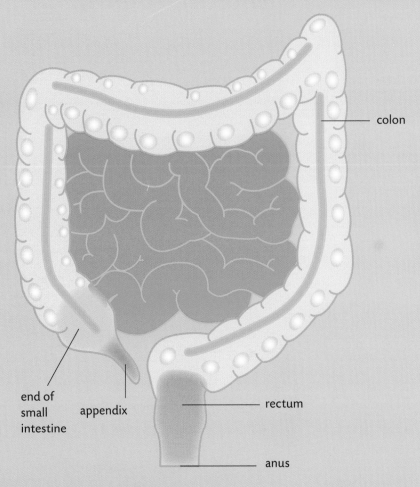

colon

The large intestine is a square shape. It is known as the colon, except for the appendix at the beginning, and the rectum at the end.

end of small intestine

appendix

rectum

anus

Through the Colon

Liquid food spends three to five hours in the small intestine, and then it goes into the large intestine. The main part of the large intestine is the colon, a muscular tube about 5 feet (1.5 m) long. The lining of the colon absorbs salt and water from the liquid chyme, making it more and more solid, and turning it into feces. The lining also makes mucus to help feces move along the tube.

Having a Bowel Movement

The muscles in the wall of the colon take turns contracting. These contractions

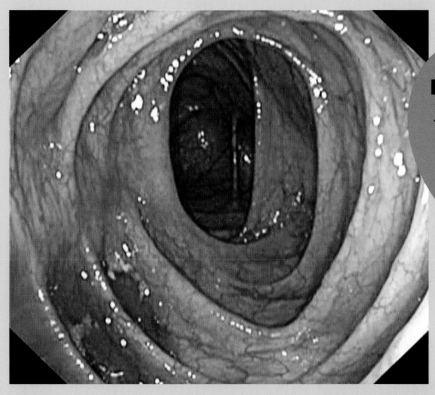

Did You Know?

Your colon can absorb about 2 quarts (2 L) of water every day.

The colon absorbs salt and water, then passes waste to the rectum.

churn up the feces and move them along. The feces can spend from ten hours to several days in the colon.

Two or three times a day, strong contractions push a large mass of feces into the rectum. The feces are stored until you feel the urge to have a bowel movement. Then, muscles in the rectum and the anus squeeze feces from your body.

What's In Your Feces?

Feces contain many things that your body can't absorb, such as fiber from the cell walls of the plants we eat. They also contain mucus, dead blood cells, and the bodies of good bacteria.

Your Appendix

A small, finger-like pouch hangs down at the start of your large intestine— this is your **appendix**. Humans don't use theirs, but animals do.

A cow uses its appendix to break down the food it eats. If your appendix becomes inflamed, it is called appendicitis. This is fixed with surgery.

Storing and Using Fuel

Your blood takes the glucose you absorb to your liver, where it is stored. It also carries glucose to all the cells of your body. Every second, your brain checks the amount of glucose in your blood to make sure it has enough.

Liver Store

Your liver is like a chemical factory in your body. Anything you don't need immediately is taken there and stored. Glucose, for example, is your body's fuel. But if there's too much in your blood, then your liver removes it and stores it as a complex carbohydrate, called glycogen. When your body exercises and needs more glucose, your liver releases some of its store into your bloodstream.

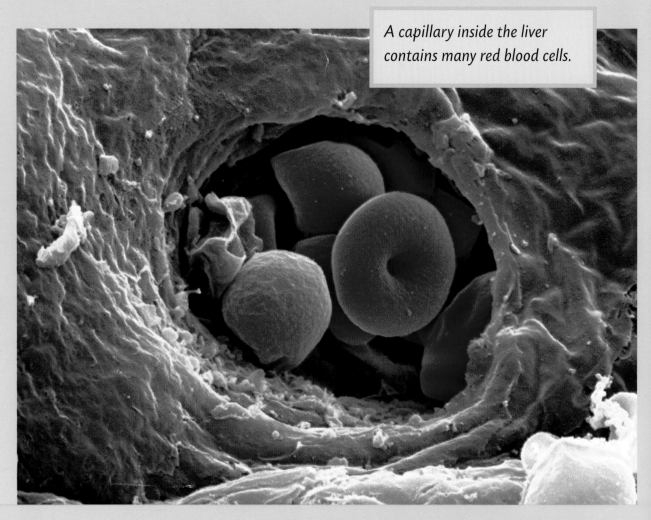

A capillary inside the liver contains many red blood cells.

WHEN THINGS GO WRONG

Diabetes

People who have a problem with producing or using insulin may have a condition called diabetes. They are diabetics and some of them need to take insulin regularly, usually by giving themselves an injection. They also need to be careful about what they eat and drink, so they can control the level of glucose in their blood. If this level rises too high, they may lose consciousness and slip into a **coma**.

A diabetic boy gives himself insulin using a pen-like device.

Glucose Control

The level of glucose in your blood is controlled by chemicals called **hormones**. Your pancreas produces a hormone called **insulin** and releases it into your bloodstream. If you have too much glucose in your blood, insulin helps your liver to store it. If your muscle cells need extra energy, then insulin helps them take glucose from your blood.

When the cells of your body need to burn more glucose, two other hormones, called adrenaline and glucagon, are released into your bloodstream. Both of them help the liver break down some of its store of glycogen into glucose.

Did You Know?

The liver is the only organ inside the body that can grow back, or regenerate, itself. You only need about a quarter of a liver to grow a whole one—but it takes several years!

Oxygen for Energy

Your cells need oxygen to help them burn glucose and release energy. Your lungs are perfectly designed to release oxygen into your blood. Breathing in and out is something your body does automatically, and yet it is one of the most important things your body does.

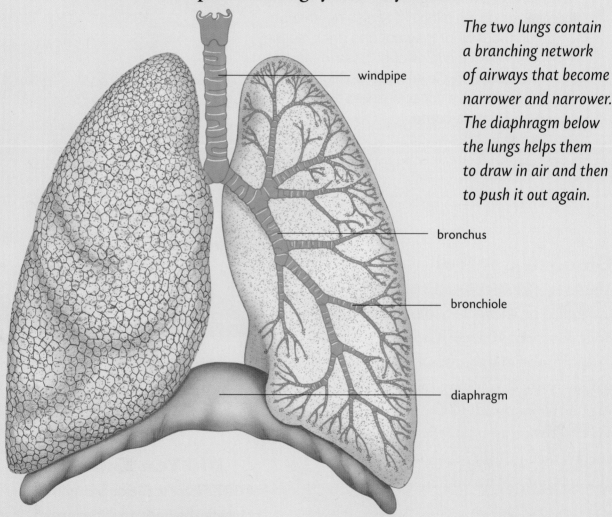

The two lungs contain a branching network of airways that become narrower and narrower. The diaphragm below the lungs helps them to draw in air and then to push it out again.

windpipe

bronchus

bronchiole

diaphragm

How Your Lungs Work

Your lungs are protected by your ribs, which form a kind of cage around them. Below the lungs is a very thick muscle, called the **diaphragm** (di-e-fram). When your diaphragm and the muscles between your ribs contract, you breathe air in. When they relax, you breathe air out.

The Movement of Air

When you're sitting still, you breathe air in and out between 12 and 15 times

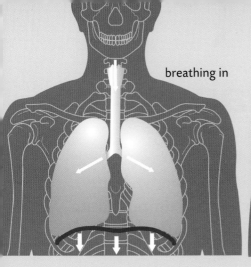
breathing in

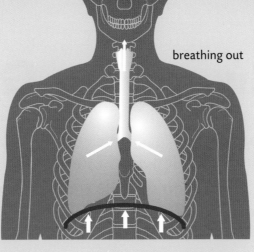
breathing out

When you breathe in (far left), air fills your lungs as the diaphragm moves down. When the diaphragm moves up (near left), air leaves the lungs.

a minute. Every time you breathe in, you take in about 1 pint (500 ml) of air. The air moves down your windpipe and into your lungs through two narrower tubes called **bronchi**. Each bronchus tube branches again and again into smaller and smaller tubes called **bronchioles**.

Eventually, the air finds its way to millions of tiny air sacs, called **alveoli** (al-vee-oh-lee). These little sacs have very thin walls, and are close to tiny blood vessels called **capillaries**. There are as many as 150 million alveoli in each lung.

Damp Lining

Your breathing tubes are kept moist by a damp lining that has millions of tiny hairs called cilia (silly-a). These hairs move mucus up to the top of your lungs, along with any particles that you may have breathed in.

Did You Know?

The network of air passages in your two lungs combined is about 1,491 miles (2,400 km) long!

HEALTH CHECK
Measuring Breathing

People who have problems breathing are regularly checked with a peak flow meter, particularly people who suffer from asthma. They take a deep breath, then breathe out as hard as they can into a wide tube. A pointer on the tube measures how much air they breathe out in liters per minute. People with asthma have narrow airways, so they breathe out less air than other people.

Swapping Gases

Once you breathe oxygen into your lungs, it needs to enter your blood so it can be delivered to every cell in your body. At the same time, the carbon dioxide that your cells have dumped into your blood goes back into your lungs to be breathed out.

Into the Blood

The oxygen in the air that you breathe in moves from your alveoli into the blood, which flows slowly through your capillaries (see page 22). There, the oxygen enters your red blood cells and sets off on its journey around your body. Carbon dioxide crosses in the opposite direction, from the capillaries and into the alveoli, where it turns into a gas and is breathed out. This swapping, or exchange, of gases is part of a process called **respiration**.

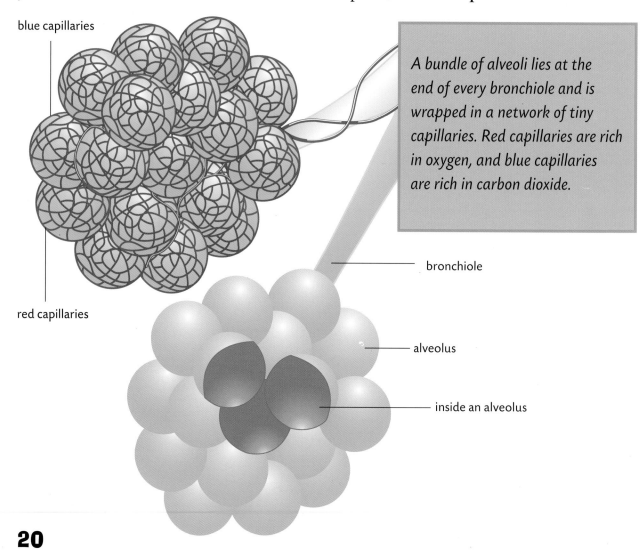

blue capillaries

red capillaries

A bundle of alveoli lies at the end of every bronchiole and is wrapped in a network of tiny capillaries. Red capillaries are rich in oxygen, and blue capillaries are rich in carbon dioxide.

bronchiole

alveolus

inside an alveolus

What's In the Air?

The air that you breathe into your lungs is mostly a gas called nitrogen. Your body doesn't need this gas, so you breathe it all out again. About a fifth of the air is made up of the oxygen your body needs. There is a small amount of carbon dioxide and tiny traces of other elements in air, too.

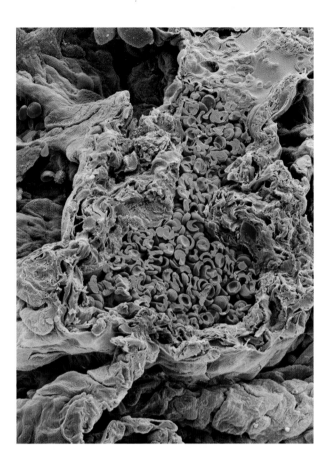

All the alveoli in the lungs are very close to thousands of red blood cells in the tiny capillaries.

A Fair Exchange

The way the gases move into and out of your blood is called **diffusion**. The air you breathe in contains more oxygen than the blood in your capillaries. Some of the oxygen diffuses, or drifts through, into your blood to make the balance equal.

At the same time, there is more carbon dioxide in the blood arriving at the lungs, so the gas passes out of your blood and into your alveoli. You then breathe it out.

What Makes You Breathe?

You would probably think that you breathe in because you don't have enough oxygen in your blood. But actually the reason you breathe in is because there's too much carbon dioxide in your blood.

Soap In the Lungs

The alveoli sacs in the lungs are very tiny and they have very thin walls. They have to stay full so they can keep exchanging gases. To do this, the lining of the sacs make a soapy substance, which stops them from collapsing like empty balloons and filling up with fluid.

Making Energy in Your Cells

Every cell in your body needs oxygen and glucose from your blood. They find their way out of your blood vessels and across each cell's wall, or **membrane**. Once inside the cell, they are taken to special power stations and are used to make energy.

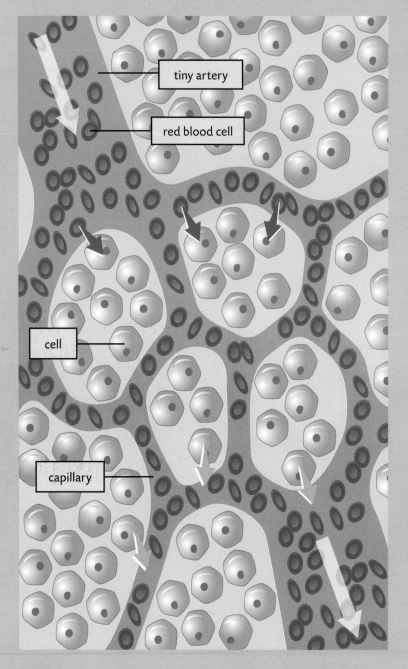

tiny artery

red blood cell

cell

capillary

Thin Capillaries

The blood has to be very close to the cells before it can release its cargo of oxygen and glucose. Your big blood vessels, called arteries, branch into smaller and smaller ones until their walls are very thin. The tiniest blood vessels with very thin walls are called capillaries.

The blood flows through the capillaries much more slowly than through the arteries, so there's plenty of time to transfer the oxygen and the glucose.

Blood flows through a tiny artery (white arrow) that branches into many capillaries. Red blood cells deliver oxygen to the cells (red arrows), while carbon dioxide leaves the cells (green arrows) and enters the bloodstream.

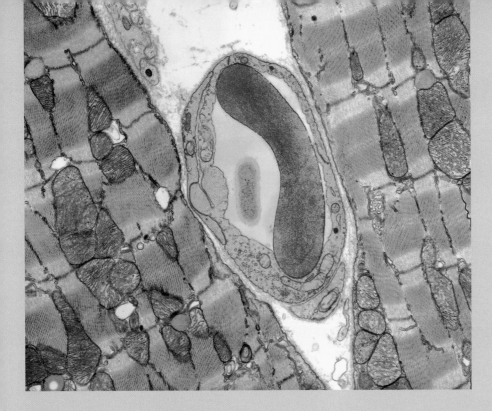

A red blood cell (bright red) squeezes through a capillary (orange) as it delivers oxygen to the cells in heart muscle (green).

Coming and Going

The membrane around a cell controls all the chemicals that enter and leave. Oxygen easily crosses the membrane, but glucose needs the help of a hormone called insulin, which is made in your pancreas and released into your blood. The insulin allows the glucose to travel through the cell membrane.

Power Stations

Every cell has a nucleus and sausage-shaped structures where chemical reactions take place. They are called mitochondria (my-toe-kon-dree-ah). Here, the oxygen and glucose help produce lots of chemical energy, and some heat energy.

The cell either uses the chemical energy or stores it until it is needed, while the heat energy warms the cell. At the same time, the mitochondria make carbon dioxide and water as waste products.

The number of mitochondria in a cell depends on how much energy it needs. A liver cell may have 2,000 because it needs to power lots of chemical reactions, but a skin cell may have less than 100.

A mitochondrion contains many folds where energy is made from glucose.

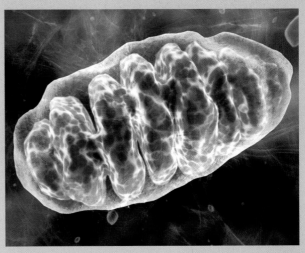

Your Energy Needs

Your body needs a certain amount of energy every day just to stay alive. Very active people need to make more energy than others. Energy comes from different types of food, and we measure it in **calories**.

Who Needs the Most Energy?

We all need different amounts of energy. Children and teenagers need more calories from their food than adults, because they are growing and are usually very active. Older people need fewer calories, because they are often less active. Pregnant women need many more calories because they are feeding the baby growing inside of them.

People who are very active use more energy than people who sit still for long periods. A football player uses far more energy than someone watching football on TV. Some people use energy faster than others, so they need more energy from their food.

How Many Calories?

Scientists have calculated the number of calories we need to eat every day. In

Children and teenagers are very active and need lots of calories to provide them with energy.

Pregnant women need more calories in their food because they are eating for two people.

general, men burn more calories than women, and babies and children need more as they grow bigger.

Babies up to five months old need about 650 calories a day. Toddlers from one to three years old need to eat about 1,300 calories a day and children between four and six need about 1,800 calories.

Seven- to ten-year-olds need about 2,000 calories a day. Girls from 11 to 14 need around 2,200 calories a day, while boys the same age need about 2,500 calories a day.

Calories from Food

Foods vary in the amount of calories they contain. Vegetables have very few, but cooking oil and other fats contain lots of calories. The amount of energy in a food depends on how much water it contains, and whether it is rich in carbohydrates, fat, or protein. These chemicals allow you to make different amounts of energy. One gram of carbohydrate or protein gives you four calories, while one gram of fat gives you nine calories.

Body Heat

Your body's cells produce heat energy all the time, particularly your muscle and liver cells. This heat helps keep your body temperature normal at 98.6°F (37°C).

Warm-Blooded

Making energy produces heat in your body. The many chemical reactions that take place in your liver cells produce lots of heat. Every time your muscles contract, they produce heat. The heat from your liver and muscle cells warms your blood as it passes through them.

If your temperature falls, your body burns more fuel and produces more energy to bring your temperature back to normal. Humans are warm-blooded animals, because we can keep our body temperature steady. Other warm-blooded animals include gorillas, monkeys, chimps, and birds.

Muscle Energy

Even when you are sitting down or standing still, you are using your muscles. You

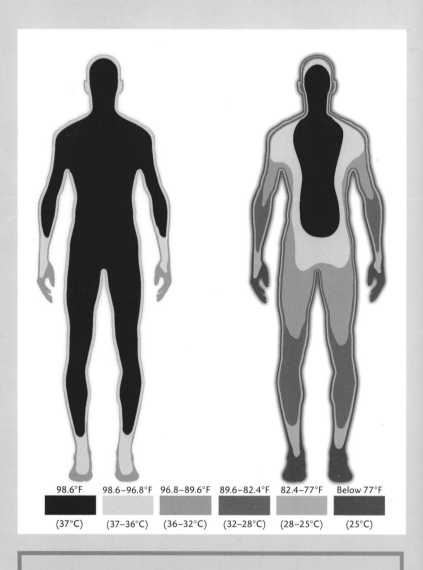

98.6°F	98.6–96.8°F	96.8–89.6°F	89.6–82.4°F	82.4–77°F	Below 77°F
(37°C)	(37–36°C)	(36–32°C)	(32–28°C)	(28–25°C)	(25°C)

A heat picture, called a thermogram, of two men. The man on the left is warm, and has a normal body temperature of 98.6°F (37°C). The man on the right is very cold, but his body still keeps his brain and his central organs at the normal temperature.

Cramps

Have you ever had a cramp? It can make a muscle feel like a painful knot. This can happen if you play a sport, such as soccer, for a long time. When the cells in your muscles run out of oxygen, they can still make energy and keep going for a short time, but they produce a chemical which collects in the muscle. This makes the muscle seem to seize up, which causes a cramp.

Soccer players often suffer cramps in the big calf muscles at the back of their legs. To relieve a cramp, they lie down with their leg in the air while someone stretches the muscle.

use your diaphragm and rib muscles to breathe, and the muscles of your skeleton to keep your body upright. When you exercise or play a sport, your muscles use a lot more energy.

When you become very hot, your blood carries heat energy away from the places it is made to the surface of your skin, where it escapes from your body. This is why you look hot after exercise. Your skin also produces sweat, which helps to cool you.

Fight or Flight

When you are in danger, your body immediately prepares to react to the danger: you might fight it or run from it! When this happens, a chemical, called adrenaline, speeds up your breathing and heart rate, and triggers the release of glucose fuel for your muscles to use.

27

Too Little or Too Much Food

Many people don't have enough to eat, and suffer from malnutrition and starvation. At the same time, more and more people in developed countries, such as the United States and the United Kingdom, eat too much and are becoming **obese**.

Not Enough Food

What happens to your body if you don't eat enough food to provide the energy and nutrients it needs? People who don't have enough to eat have little energy because their cells don't receive the glucose they need.

Instead, their bodies burn their stores of fat and their muscles. As a result, they grow thinner, lose weight, and feel very tired. When all their fat has been burned, their bodies start to burn the protein in their cells. This is very dangerous, and they may die.

People with malnutrition are not eating the proteins, fats, vitamins, and minerals they need to lead healthy lives. This means that they are more likely to catch infections because their bodies aren't strong enough to resist illness.

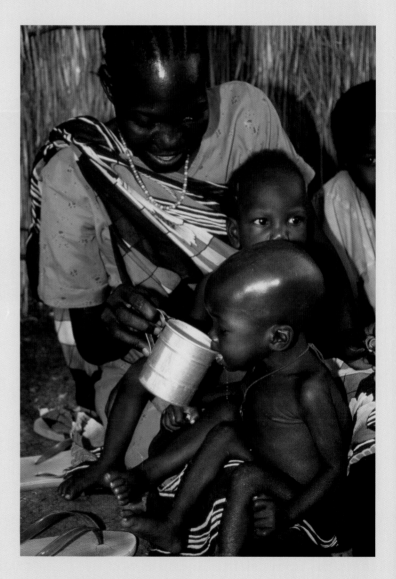

A Sudanese mother feeds her malnourished child enriched milk.

Too Much Food

What happens to your body if you eat too many calories? You put on weight. If you continue eating too many calories, you may become fat and overweight. Very overweight people are called obese.

Some people put on weight more easily than others. How much you should weigh depends on how tall you are and how old you are. If you always eat more calories than you burn, your body will turn the food into fat and store it in various parts of your body, increasing your weight.

The best way to lose weight is to exercise regularly and to cut down on foods that contain a lot of fat and sugar.

Teenagers who are overweight or obese take part in a special fitness class to help them lose weight.

PROBLEMS WITH DAIRY FOODS

Some people get stomach pains and diarrhea when they drink milk or eat dairy foods (foods that contain milk). This is a problem with their digestive system, which is called lactose intolerance. It means their system can't digest lactose, the natural sugar found in milk. These people have to avoid eating dairy products for the rest of their lives.

Glossary

alveoli   Tiny air sacs in the lungs where oxygen enters the blood, and carbon dioxide leaves the blood.

anorexia   An illness in which a person stops eating because they are afraid of getting fat.

appendix   A small, finger-like pouch hanging down at the start of the large intestine.

bacteria   A huge group of single-celled microorganisms. Some types of bacteria cause serious diseases.

bile   A liquid that helps to break down fats.

bronchi   Airways that branch off of the windpipe as it enters the lungs.

bronchioles   Airways that branch off of the bronchi inside the lungs.

calorie   A unit of energy contained in food.

capillary   A tiny blood vessel that carries blood to the cells of the body.

carbohydrate   Chemicals that provide energy. Complex carbohydrates are an energy store, and simple carbohydrates are burned to make energy.

chyme   Half-digested food produced in the stomach.

coma   When a person loses consciousness, they slip into a coma.

diaphragm   The sheet-like, powerful muscle under the lungs that helps them breathe air in and out.

diffusion   A movement of a chemical from one place to another.

digestive system   The parts of the body, from the mouth to the large intestine, where food is broken down and absorbed into the blood.

esophagus   Part of the digestive system, which connects your mouth to your stomach.

fats   Greasy solids and liquids, such as margarines and oils, in food.

gallbladder   An organ near the liver that stores bile.

glucose   A simple sugar that the body's cells need for generating energy.

glycogen   A complex carbohydrate that is a store of glucose in the liver.

hormone   One of the chemicals that act as messengers in the body. Hormones help control the way the body works and develops.

insulin   A hormone that helps glucose enter cells and to be stored as glycogen in the liver.

lactose   A simple sugar found in milk and dairy products.

malnutrition An illness that results from lack of food, or eating an unhealthy diet.

membrane A very thin layer that may be found inside a cell, around a cell, or as a protective covering for a row of cells.

metabolism The process by which the body breaks down and builds up molecules.

molecule A single unit of particle of certain chemicals.

mucus A liquid made by the body to stop membranes from drying out.

obese Having excessive body fat.

proteins Chemicals that are essential for cells to grow and work.

respiration The process of breathing in oxygen and breathing out carbon dioxide.

saliva A fluid that stops the mouth from drying out, and also helps break down carbohydrates in food.

salivary glands Three glands in the mouth that secrete saliva.

starch A complex carbohydrate found in food, such as potatoes.

sucrose A simple sugar found in sugar cane.

vitamins Nutrients that are essential for health.

Further Reading

My Body. World Book, 2008.
Claybourne, Anna. *The Human Body*. Chelsea House, 2006.
Walker, Richard. *Human Body*. New York DK, 2009.

Web Sites

www.biology4kids.com/files/cell_mito.html
Find out more about energy-producing mitochondria.

www.keepkidshealthy.com/index.html
Find out more about energy needs, diet, and body weight.

www.biology4kids.com/files/systems_digestive.html
Find out more about how your digestive system works.

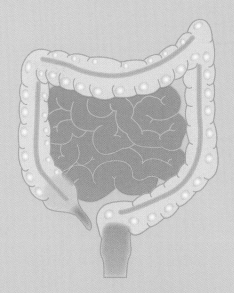

Index

absorption 12–13
adrenaline 17, 27
alveoli 19, 20, 21
anorexia 9
appendix 14, 15
appetite 9

bacteria 11, 13, 15
bile 11
blood 5, 6, 8, 9, 12, 13,
    16, 17, 18, 19, 20, 21,
    22, 23, 26, 27
brain 4, 9, 26
breathing 4, 5, 6, 18–19,
    20, 21, 27
bronchi 18, 19
bronchiole 18, 19, 20

calorie 7, 24–25, 28, 29
capillary 16, 19, 20, 21,
    22, 23
carbohydrates 5, 6–7, 8,
    10, 16, 25
carbon dioxide 6, 20–21,
    22, 23
cells 4, 5, 6, 7, 16, 17, 18,
    20, 22–23, 26, 27, 28
chyme 11, 12, 14
colon 13, 14, 15
coma 17

diabetes 17
diaphragm 18, 19, 27

diffusion 21
digestion 5, 8, 9,
    10–11, 12
digestive system 9, 10–11

esophagus 10
exercise 5, 16, 27, 29

fats 5, 7, 8, 11, 13, 25,
    28, 29
feces 13, 14, 15
food 4, 5, 6, 7, 8, 9, 10,
    11, 12, 24, 25, 28–29

gallbladder 10, 11
glucose 5, 6, 7, 13, 16, 17,
    18, 22, 23, 27, 28
glycogen 6, 7, 16, 17

heat 23, 26–27
hormone 17, 23
hunger 8–9

insulin 17, 23

lactose 7, 29
large intestine 10, 12, 13,
    14, 15
liver 4, 6, 10, 12, 16, 17,
    23, 26
lungs 4, 18–19, 20, 21

malnutrition 7, 28

membrane 22, 23
metabolism 5
mitochondria 23
molecules 5
mucus 11, 14, 15, 19
muscles 4, 7, 8, 10, 14,
    15, 17, 18, 26, 27, 28

obesity 28, 29
oxygen 5, 6, 18–19,
    20–21, 22, 23, 27

pancreas 10, 11, 17, 23
proteins 5, 7, 8, 25, 28

red blood cells 16, 20,
    21, 22, 23
respiration 18–19, 20

saliva 6, 10, 11
small intestine 10, 11, 12,
    14
starch 6, 10
stomach 6, 8, 9, 10, 11
sucrose 7
sugar 4, 5, 6, 7, 9, 13

temperature 26

vitamins 5, 13, 28

waste 14–15, 23
water 5, 6, 12, 14, 15, 23

CC

Central Childrens